Learning to Pray Again

Peace and joy through an ancient practice

Michael Rinehart

Contents

Introduction

When I look at your heavens, the work of your fingers,
the moon and the stars that you have established;
what are human beings that you are mindful of them,
mortals that you care for them?

—Psalm 8:3-4

Everybody prays. If you've ever hoped that a date would say "Yes," that you would get a good grade on the paper, get the job offer, dodge a diagnosis, then you have prayed. The yearning of the heart is prayer.

If you have ever stood on a mountaintop, overwhelmed by the beauty, or at the ocean, struck by its majesty, or laid in your backyard staring at the stars, millions of miles away, you have prayed.

If you have sat or walked in silence, allowing your spirit to become calm and receptive, if you have listened to your soul, discerned an important decision, or if you have felt a tug within you to do something benevolent, bigger than yourself, then you have prayed. You have experienced what people throughout the ages have called the Holy Spirit. You have communed with God.

Even if you feel far from God right now, God is closer than you think, closer than a brother, closer than your own skin. God is in you and around you, in every breath you take.

Prayer is multifaceted. There are many different ways to pray. Some of these ways are more conducive to your personality than others. There have been many times in my life that I have been stuck in my prayer life. For one reason or another I felt I couldn't even pray. Most often, it was discovering a new way of praying that helped me break through to a new place of deeper peace, greater awareness and more acute introspection.

This small book is a prayer journey. In these 40 chapters we will explore many different ways to pray. If you read these each day, I guarantee you will find all kinds of ways to pray. You will not be bored. If you're stuck, you will get unstuck. Try it. Ideas for using this as a series or small group study are in Appendix B.

I encourage you to read a chapter a day, and try some of the exercises in these pages each day. Take notes. Start a prayer journal. If something works particularly well, make a note of it. If something doesn't work for you at all, write it down. It might not be the right thing at this moment, but what about twenty years down the road? It might be just what you need.

1

Some Benefits of Prayer - Strength

The Lord gives power to the faint, and strengthens the powerless.
Even youths will faint and be weary,
and the young will fall exhausted;
but those who wait for the Lord shall renew their strength,
they shall mount up with wings like eagles,
they shall run and not be weary,
they shall walk and not faint.

—Isaiah 40:29-31

I once asked a group to write down as many reasons they could think of to pray. Anything goes. Let's begin our conversations and experiences of prayer with this same exercise. Grab a fresh notebook for these next few weeks. Consider it your prayer journal. Write today's date, and then: "Why Pray?" Then consider this question: "If I took 30 minutes a day to pray, every day, what might be some of the benefits, intended and unintended?"

Ready? Go...

When you have finished your list, look at some of the responses I have heard over the years to these questions, all of them true in my experience. Read these slowly and consider if any of them are true for you.

"I believe I'd have more peace."

"It might calm me down."

"I believe it would help me listen for God's voice more acutely."

"It would give me more time to reflect on my life and my relationships."

"It would refocus me on what is important in life."

"I believe it would make me more attuned to and available for others."

"It would deepen my faith."

"It would give me more focus and energy."

"When I pray in the morning it sets my day on the right foot."

"When I pray in the morning, I am more likely to pray during the day."

"I want to grow spiritually."

"Prayer lowers my anxiety."

Martin Marty is a prolific writer. I once asked him what was the secret to his productivity. Without missing a beat he said he took a short catnap every day. Even in his office, he would lay down midday and take time to rest. Sometimes, getting off the treadmill of life renews our strength.

The passage from Isaiah above puts it well. Those who wait on the Lord will renew their strength. I have found most people don't think of prayer as a way to regain strength. If you're tired or if your spirit is worn down, consider prayer as a way of building yourself back up.

2

Some Benefits of Prayer – Joy

Rejoice in the Lord always; again I will say, Rejoice. Let your gentleness be known to everyone. The Lord is near. Do not worry about anything, but in everything by prayer and supplication with thanksgiving let your requests be made known to God. And the peace of God, which surpasses all understanding, will guard your hearts and your minds in Christ Jesus.

—Philippians 4:4-7

If you are anxious, know that one of the benefits of prayer is lower anxiety. This may not be the primary purpose of prayer, but it is a valuable unintended consequence. Prayer primarily is communion with God. It deepens our spiritual life. I find it interesting, nevertheless, that the apostle Paul connects prayer and anxiety in the passage above. "Do not worry" is "Have no anxiety about anything" in some translations. Paul connects battling fear, worry and anxiety with prayer and thanksgiving.

For your prayer exercise today, find a comfortable place to sit and write in your prayer journal. Write the date, and then the word "Worries." Read the Philippians passage above and take some time for silence. Then make a list of your greatest fears and worries. What keeps you up at night? Keep writing until you can't think of anything else.

Take your time. You may think that listing your fears would increase them. In most cases the opposite happens. Our fears often feel amorphous, overwhelming. Seeing them written on a finite piece of paper often puts them in perspective. Next, go down your list, item by item, and turn these things over to God. It is true that some things are in our hands. I have at times been the author of my own demise. Most things in life are out of our hands. Life and death, how others act, the economy – most of these things are out of our control. It is best just to give them to God.

Now make another list entitled, "Joys." Before, you listed the things that keep you up at night. Now list the things that get you up in the morning. What revs your engine? What makes your pulse rate go up and your heart sing?

When you are done, take time to dwell on this list, and give these things to God as well. Your prayer life can lower your anxiety and increase your joy. The root word of "rejoice" is "joy." Read the entire letter to the Philippians and count the number of times Paul uses the words "joy" and "rejoice." Did you know that Paul wrote this letter from a prison cell?

Make a commitment to setting aside time for prayer. Make it a gift to yourself, to increase your joy. The benefits will be enormous. You'll be glad you did.

3

Give Thanks

If the only prayer you ever say in your entire life is thank you,
it will be enough.

—Meister Eckhardt

Meister Eckhardt was a 14th century German mystic. His statement speaks for itself. He invites us to have an attitude of gratitude in our prayers.

One can focus on what one lacks, or one can focus on what one has. A cornerstone of spiritual awareness, mindfulness, is becoming aware of how much of life is a marvelous gift. I did not ask to be born. I did not earn it. It is a free gift. My body is a wonderful gift, even with its flaws. My talents are a gift from God. Everything we have is a gift. Enter your day today with a profound sense of how every relationship is sacred. Every mundane task is an act of love.

For what are you thankful? In your prayers today, take a moment to take stock. Write "I am thankful for" in your prayer journal and make a list. My life. My spouse. My kids. My house. My health. My work. My friends. The earth. The sky. The trees. The stars. The sun shining on my face. The wind. The air I'm breathing. The list can go on for a long time if you think about it deeply. Please do.

Focusing your heart and mind on these things puts life in perspective. You will see the world differently. We often spend our time thinking about what we don't have. No matter how much we have, there will always be some things we don't have. By dwelling on those things, they become larger than life, and we become blind to the universe of things right in front of our eyes.

When you are finished with your list, read back through it, slowly. Offer a prayer of thanks for each thing. Carry this awareness of the gift of life into your life today. Some people begin each day of their lives with this prayer. According to Eckhardt, if this was the only prayer you ever prayed, it would be enough.

4

Take Stock of Your Prayer Life

Seven times a day I praise you for your righteous ordinances.

—Psalm 119:164

I was once asked to speak to a group of young pastors about prayer from a personal standpoint. They didn't want boilerplate theories. They wanted to know what had actually worked. What didn't work? What do you do when you get stuck? Give us a realistic picture of a prayer life in the real world.

I took the opportunity to think about the ups and downs of my own prayer life over the years. Frankly, it's been a roller coaster. There were times when I hardly prayed at all, when my old prayer patterns no longer worked. I outgrew them. Eventually, with help from pastors and spiritual directors, I learned new ways of praying. There were times when faith bloomed. My prayer life was rich and diverse. There are seasons of life. Sometimes there is a rich harvest. Other times the fields lie fallow. We need different forms of prayer for different seasons.

So let's get started. We've already jumped into some prayers, and have started a prayer journal. Let's start today by praying about praying. Take time to consider your current beliefs and practices of prayer. Think also about what you might like them to be moving forward.

It will not do to race into a conversation about prayer frenetically. Sit quietly for 30 minutes and think about this. Consider taking some notes in a journal or simple spiral notebook. Perhaps go for a long walk. Consider the following questions during your reflection time:

What does my prayer life look like now? In the past? Who taught me to pray, if anyone? What works? What no longer works? How often do I pray? When? What do I believe about prayer? Where do I find myself praying? When in the rhythm of my day am I quiet, reflective? When could I be quiet, given the demands of my life? How do I pray? Out loud? Silently? Alone? With others? Do I pray differently today than I did ten years ago? What would I like my prayer life to be like? Why? How do I commune with God? When have I experienced God most profoundly in my life?

Reflecting on these questions is a form of prayer. Take it slow. Give yourself the gift of time. There is no hurry. This is praying with the mind. It is asking yourself and God how your prayer life and spiritual life might be ordered.

When in your day could you set aside some time for prayer? Morning, afternoon, evening? You'll need a block of time for reflection. You can start with 15 minutes, but you'll soon discover it won't be enough. You'll want 30 minutes, and eventually an hour. When might this happen?

Let these questions be on your mind all day, and into the week. Find someone with whom you can discuss these things. Ask them about their own experience with prayer. Save your reflections in your journal, so you can come back and revisit them later, after you've worked through the exercises in this book. Give yourself this gift of time, at least once a day, if not seven times a day as the psalmist recounts.

5

Silence

The fruit of silence is prayer
the fruit of prayer is faith
the fruit of faith is love
the fruit of love is service
the fruit of service is peace.

—Mother Teresa

Silence is prayer.

As a child, I often thought of prayer as talking with God. Even if we embrace this metaphor, if one is talking with another, shouldn't it be at least 50% listening? Furthermore, if the other with whom one is talking is God, shouldn't it be more like 60% or 70% listening? If you were getting golf coaching from Tiger Woods, would you spend most of your time talking or listening?

In his book *On Becoming a Magical Mystical Bear,* Matthew Fox points out that most of us learned to pray as children, in a formative stage of our lives when we were dependent on our parents for everything. For this reason our praying can turn into a litany of all the things that we want. We treat God like a celestial Santa Claus. Then, somewhere in adolescence we become arrested in our spiritual development. We never learned to pray as adults.

What if we began renewing our prayer life with silence? Let God speak. Listen.

If you're stuck in your prayer life, then begin with silence. If listening is prayer, and if silence is prayer, then perhaps prayer is communion with God, not just talking.

Go for a long walk. 30 minutes. Take no music or reading with you. Just walk. Notice your steps, your breathing. Look at the earth, the trees, the sky. Breathe it in. Let go. Let God be.

Or find a comfortable place in your home where you can sit uninterrupted for a time. Set a notepad or prayer journal and a pen on the table next to you. Put your feet flat on the ground. Rest your arms comfortably on your lap. Close your eyes and listen to your breathing. Let it slow. Invite God to sit with you.

Resist the urge to say anything. If you're like most people, your mind will race with thoughts of the day. It's alright. If you're like me, you'll start thinking, perhaps obsessing about things you're supposed to get done. I forgot to make that doctor's appointment or to get the oil changed. When those to-do list items rise to the surface, simply write them down on your notepad and go back to your quiet.

In time, your thoughts and worries will settle like the impurities in a glass of water, and things will become clear. This may be difficult at first, if you're not accustomed to it, but that's okay. You're just getting started.

6

Lectio Divina

*Keep these words that I am commanding you today in your heart.
Recite them to your children and talk about them when you are at
home and when you are away, when you lie down and when you rise.
Bind them as a sign on your hand, fix them as an emblem on your
forehead, and write them on the doorposts of your house
and on your gates.*

—Deuteronomy 6:6-9

Lectio divina is an ancient spiritual way to pray, taught by Christian monks. *Lectio divina* is a Latin phrase that simply means "divine reading." *Lectio* was one of four patterns of prayer in the monastic tradition: *lectio divina, oratio, meditatio,* and *contemplatio.* We will talk about the others in the next chapters.

In *lectio divina*, we pray by reading, reflecting, responding and resting. Most people have experienced the meditative effects of reading. You don't, however, have to be an avid reader to benefit from this kind of prayer. In fact, it's better with a short passage of Scripture. Here's how it works.

Read a passage from the Bible. Read the passage several times with space to ponder it in between each reading. Consider for example the story of the prodigal son, Luke 15:11-32. Read slowly. Reflect. Who are you in the story? Have you sometimes been the younger son, wandering far from home, participating in self-destructive behavior? When? Have you sometimes been the father, having to offer forgiveness? When? Have you at times been the self-righteous older brother? When? Next consider how you might respond to the text in your life. Then simply be at rest. Some call this "dwelling in the Word."

Lectio Divina can be done by yourself or in a group. When done as a group, it can involve conversation. Before reading the text, invite people to listen for a word or phrase that strikes them. Have someone read the text, then let people offer a word or phrase that caught their attention.

Before the second reading, ask listeners to focus their attention on how the passage speaks to their life that day. Have another voice read the passages a second time. After a time of quiet let people share their thoughts on what the passage has to say to us.

Then invite people to contemplate these questions: "What action would I take this week if I were to take this passage seriously? What does this mean for how I live my life today? Tomorrow?" Have another voice read the passage a third time, then discuss. The advantage of doing Bible study like this is it requires no expert, no top-down teaching. The lesson emerges from the group, prayerfully.

You can do this by yourself, or in a group. The point is letting the text wash over you. Rather than you studying it, let it study you, shape you. This kind of divine reading is also prayer.

7

Oratio – Intercessory Prayer

Ask, and it will be given to you; search, and you will find; knock,
and the door will be opened for you. For everyone who asks
receives, and everyone who searches finds, and for everyone who
knocks, the door will be opened.

—Matthew 7:7-8

"Ask, and it will be given to you..." These are the words of Jesus.
Like every Rabbi, he taught his disciples to pray. Jesus invites us to
ask for the desires of our hearts. We won't always get what we want,
but when you go searching you will find something for your soul.
Discovery always begins with seeking.

Oratio is the second of the four Monastic forms of prayer. *Oratio* is
also a Latin word. It means to pray or to plead. It is the word from
which we get our word "oration." *Oratio* is a form of spoken prayer.
This is what most people think of when they think of praying. It's
also what most often happens in church. While God is not a celestial
Santa Claus, Jesus portrays God as a loving parent, who wishes to
give us the very best.

There are several ways to go about this. In this chapter, I will talk
about intercessory prayer. In the next chapter, I will talk about rote
prayers. In the following chapter, we will discuss extemporaneous
prayer.

Intercessory prayer is about praying for what we need for ourselves
or for others. My mother used to keep a notebook. She probably still
does. When someone asks her to pray for them, or for someone else,

she does not respond with glib affirmation and then forget about it. She writes it in her book and remembers it in her morning prayers. Generally this will continue until she is told to stop. Her list gets long.

As a pastor I prayed for the members of my congregation, using the membership directory. As a bishop, I pray for our congregations, pastors and leaders. At first I found I could get through this rather quickly. As I got to know them, each name called to mind people and situations that got my mind spinning. I used to pray for our 100+ congregations a day. Then it became 100+ congregations a week. Now it seems to take longer, as I spend time thinking and praying about each situation.

Being mindful of those we love can take time. Each day can begin with a prayer of thanks for life. Then I pray for my spouse and my children. Next my parents, then my brother and sister and their family. Where does one stop? Then I will pray for the staff, my coworkers. Then I have a list of prayer concerns that have been brought to me by all the aforementioned folks.

For some people this systematic kind of prayer makes the most sense. It's tangible, practical and important. It almost requires that you have a notebook or a prayer journal. These days I keep notes in my phone, so my prayer list is with me at all times, walking, at work, at church or at home.

Start by writing out your prayer list. Who would you want to remember in prayer daily?

8

Oratio – Rote or Memorized Prayers

*Almighty and everlasting God,
you have brought us in safety to this new day.
Preserve us with your mighty power, that we may not fall into sin
nor be overcome in adversity. In all we do, direct us to the fulfilling
of your purpose; through Jesus Christ our Lord.*

The prayer above is part of the traditional Morning Prayer service. Many people pray it daily. Some prayers are so elegant and powerful they are repeated often. The Lord's Prayer. The Serenity Prayer. The Prayer of St. Francis. These prayers say what we want to say when we cannot find the words. After decades of praying these prayers, they become part of us. We even refer to memorization as learning something "by heart."

"Rote" means mechanical or habitual repetition of something to be learned. For many, that means memorized, like the Lord's Prayer. While memorizing prayers is a good thing, I am also using the word to refer to any kind of spoken prayer, written, read, or memorized.

When you find a prayer that embodies something you want to say, in the way you'd like to say it, write it in your journal and make it part of your daily prayer habit. If a prayer is important to you, and you pray it daily, it won't be long before it is memorized.

In Appendix A is a list of some prayers, one per month, to broaden your prayer vocabulary. You might consider making them part of your repertoire.

Of course the most common rote prayer of the Christian tradition is the prayer Jesus taught his disciples to pray. We know it as the Lord's Prayer or the Our Father. Most Christians have memorized this prayer and can pray it "by heart." Far from seeing God as an angry judge or power-hungry tyrant, Jesus taught his followers this humble prayer which addresses God as a loving Father. The original language actually means "daddy." In his Small Catechism, the German church reformer Martin Luther encouraged his followers to pray this prayer first thing in the morning and just before bed.

Why not make this prayer part of your daily ritual? Try it today. Pray it slowly, petition by petition. Dwell on passages that move you. "Give us this day our daily bread." What do you need? "Forgive us our trespasses…" For what do you need forgiveness? "…as we forgive those who trespass against us." Who needs your forgiveness? Make this your own prayer.

Some fear rote prayers because they can seem dry. One can go through the motions. Consider this. Does saying "I love you" get old? I suppose it could, and yet it's so important. Some things need to become rote in our lives. What things need to become permanent parts of your prayer life?

9

Oratio – **Extemporized Prayer**

I know, I know. We are Your chosen people.
But, once in a while, can't You choose someone else?

—Tevye, in *Fiddler on the Roof*

Extemporized prayer is another form of spoken prayer. Not a collected list of intercessions, not memorized or written prayers, but a free conversation with God. Try this while walking through your neighborhood. People will think you've lost it.

Tevye comes to mind when I think of this kind of prayer. Walking with his wheelbarrow, while he's working throughout the day, Tevye has a running conversation with God. "Would it spoil some vast, eternal plan, if I were a wealthy man?"

In one of the earliest letters of the New Testament, the apostle Paul encourages his listeners to "pray without ceasing." (1 Thessalonians 5:17) Praying in the morning focuses us on higher things. The work of the day can come barreling in and leave us out of touch with the things upon which our prayers focused us: love, forgiveness, joy, peace and so on. What might it take to remain in a prayerful posture throughout the day? Listening for God. Dwelling in Christ's peace.

Today, practice talking to God throughout the day as you work. This may be difficult, but talk to God like someone right next to you. Be honest about your frustrations and temptations. Consider how Christ might want you to treat your coworkers, even the most difficult one. How might Christ want you to treat your boss? Your employees?

One trick I've used for those who are wanting to be prayerful throughout the day is to set your phone, tablet, computer or watch alarm to go off every hour as a reminder to pray. One time a congregation passed out small circular stickers (the size of the end of a pencil eraser) for people to put on their watch or phone. Every time they saw the sticker, it reminded them to pray.

If Christ came for a visit, and you went for a walk, what might you want to discuss? And what's keeping you from doing it?

10

Meditatio

My eyes are awake before each watch of the night,
that I may meditate on your promise.

—Psalm 119:148

In his introduction to the publication of his own German writings, the church reformer Martin Luther adapted the four monastic forms of prayer, *lectio, oratio, meditatio and contemplatio,* into what he called "a correct way of studying theology." In Psalm 119 he believed King David showed us three rules: *oratio, meditatio and tentatio.* (Luther's Works 34:285) He was not proposing these as ways to pray, but rather ways to interpret Scripture theologically. The first is to pray, to seek understanding. We have covered this in the last few chapters.

The second, Luther said, is meditation, which he describes as not only in the heart, but also by repeating the Scriptures out loud. Sing, speak and hear them over and over. Luther no doubt learned this from his own experience as a monk, singing the psalms every morning.

This would not have to be a long passage of scripture. In fact, it could be quite short, a brief phrase that is repeated again and again for focus. It may be as simple as the phrase, "Lord Jesus Christ, have mercy on me." Some monastics would suggest perhaps using just a word, like, "Jesus," or "Peace." Some call this a mantra. Father Thomas Keating suggests this kind of meditation as a form of centering prayer, preparing us for contemplative prayer.

Speak your word or phrase a few times, then be silent. When the mind wanders, return to your refrain. Speak your word or phrase again, several times, then be silent. Your word or phrase becomes a focal point, calling you back to prayer. It is simply a tool to center yourself, still your mind and make you receptive to the Holy Spirit. Few of us have the ability to sit down and simply shut off our minds, opening our hearts. We are simply too distracted. A mantra can help you get there.

Try this out. Sit comfortably in your spot or go for a walk. Pick a word, phrase or a scripture passage. Here are some possibilities:

> *Lord Jesus Christ, you are the light of the world. Give me peace in my mind and joy in my heart.*

> *By this shall all people know you are my disciples, if you love one another.*

Find a phrase or verse that puts your focus where it needs to be, then repeat it over and over with periods of silence in between. Allow yourself 15 to 20 minutes of this kind of meditation. If you're doing the study in a group, take some time to share what this experience is like with others, hearing their experiences as well.

Try this kind of prayer for a week, and see what kind of fruit it bears in your life.

11

Contemplatio

Be still and know that I am God.

—Psalm 46:10

My son said to me, "Dad, it's impossible to think about nothing." This is precisely what contemplation is. Contemplation is leading the mind to rest. It is simply being with God, without the need to say or think anything at all. Some call this the purest form of prayer, where the Holy Spirit is the principal actor. We are simply receptive vessels into which God pours hope, love, peace and other gifts of the Spirit.

> *On that day you will ask nothing of me. Very truly, I tell you, if you ask anything of the Father in my name, he will give it to you. Until now you have not asked for anything in my name. Ask and you will receive, so that your joy may be complete.* (John 16:23-24)

Pure contemplation is not easy. It takes a lot of practice. St. John of the Cross said, "Pure contemplation lies in receiving." Father Thomas Keating said, "Contemplative prayer is not so much the absence of thoughts as detachment from them. It is the opening of mind and heart, body and emotions 'our whole being' to God." Hans Urs von Balthasar said, "Contemplative prayer is a conversation in which God's word has the initiative and we, for the moment, can be nothing more than listeners."

Contemplative prayer is not for passive people. Contemplative prayer is allowing ourselves to be still and silent for a time. This almost always leads to more focused and productive activity. Most contemplatives are social activists. Indeed, true activism in the world is exhausting. It would be nearly impossible without adequate time for reflection and renewal.

You may need to spend some time in meditation and other forms of prayer before contemplation will be possible, but give it a try.

The psalmist says, "Be still and know that I am God." Perhaps begin with these words, spoken slowly, taking one word off the end each time:

Be still and know that I am God.
Be still and know that I am…
Be still and know that I…
Be still and know that…
Be still and know…
Be still and…
Be still…
Be…

12

Tentatio

I am poured out like water, and all my bones are out of joint;
my heart is like wax; it is melted within my breast;
my mouth is dried up like a potsherd,
and my tongue sticks to my jaws;
you lay me in the dust of death.

—Psalm 22:14-15

I mentioned previously that the church reformer Martin Luther altered the four monastic forms of prayer, *lectio, oratio, meditatio and contemplatio,* into three rules for studying theology correctly: *oratio, meditatio and tentatio.* (Luther's Works 34:285) Luther translated *tentatio*, the third of these rules, into German with the word *Anfechtung*: temptation, challenge, dispute.

Luther describes this as the kind of distress one feels when one is oppressed or distressed. When we are suffering for any reason, or when we are anxious, Luther says prayer and God's word brings us comfort.

It is amazing how difficult times can actually bring us closer to God. When things are going well, we often begin to trust in our own self-achievement and self-sufficiency. We begin to believe the myth that we got where we are on our own. It's not until something is going badly that we realize how dependent we are, how mortal we are. This is when we are most likely to reach out to the universe for consolation, hope and meaning.

The apostle Paul once prayed that God would take away a problem that he had. This problem was so bad he called it a "thorn in the flesh." The answer was "No." It was not the answer Paul wanted to hear. "My grace is sufficient for you for my power is made perfect in weakness." (2 Corinthians 12:9)

God cares about those who suffer. I haven't decided if God draws near to us when we are hurting, or whether we are simply more aware and receptive of God's presence.

Jesus put it this way in the Beatitudes, the very first part of the Sermon on the Mount (Matthew 5:1-12):

When Jesus saw the crowds, he went up the mountain; and after he sat down, his disciples came to him. Then he began to speak, and taught them, saying:

'Blessed are the poor in spirit, for theirs is the kingdom of heaven.
'Blessed are those who mourn, for they will be comforted.
'Blessed are the meek, for they will inherit the earth.
'Blessed are those who hunger and thirst for righteousness, for they will be filled.

'Blessed are the merciful, for they will receive mercy.
'Blessed are the pure in heart, for they will see God.
'Blessed are the peacemakers, for they will be called children of God.
'Blessed are those who are persecuted for righteousness' sake, for theirs is the kingdom of heaven.

'Blessed are you when people revile you and persecute you and utter all kinds of evil against you falsely on my account. Rejoice and be glad, for your reward is great in heaven, for in the same way they persecuted the prophets who were before you.

We have to be careful here. I am not saying that God intentionally visits suffering on some and not others. That would be a capricious and cruel god. I am saying that when we are suffering, we often experience the presence of God in more profound ways.

30

So how do we practice this? No, I am not suggesting that you go out and find a way to suffer. I am suggesting that when times are hard, expect God to show up. If you want to experience this intentionally, and you yourself are not suffering, then go find someone who is. Enter into another person's suffering. Jesus promised that when we encountered those who are hungry, thirsty, naked, stranger, sick or in prison, we would encounter Jesus himself.

It may be a new idea, thinking of solidarity with those who suffer as a form of prayer, but I would leave you with this thought from the apostle Paul in Romans 12. Giving of ourselves is a form of worship.

I appeal to you therefore, brothers and sisters, by the mercies of God, to present your bodies as a living sacrifice, holy and acceptable to God, which is your spiritual worship.

13

Fasting

And whenever you fast, do not look dismal, like the hypocrites, for they disfigure their faces so as to show others that they are fasting. Truly I tell you, they have received their reward. But when you fast, put oil on your head and wash your face, so that your fasting may be seen not by others but by your Father who is in secret; and your Father who sees in secret will reward you.

—Matthew 6:16-18

Notice that Jesus says "when you fast" not "if you fast." Jesus, like many in antiquity, took fasting for granted. He assumed that his followers would fast, as people of every religion, in every culture had for ages. Fasting is good for the body and good for the soul. It cleanses the body and is also a form of prayer.

Every time I have fasted, it has been a spiritual experience. Perhaps it is coming in touch with our mortality. Or perhaps it is simply feeling hungry that draws our attention to something deeper. In any case, let us add fasting to our list of ways to pray. The season of Lent, the 40 days leading up to Easter, are focused on three disciplines: prayer, fasting and almsgiving (generosity). The latter will be taken up in the next chapter.

There are lots of different kinds of fasts. There are partial fasts and complete fasts. There are fasts from certain kinds of foods, like meat or sweets. There are fasts during the day, but not at night. Fasting is simply depriving ourselves from something for spiritual purposes. You can fast from watching television. The complete fast is the most serious kind of fast. While complete fasts can be very good for you, be sure check with your doctor before attempting a complete fast.

Many characters in the Bible fasted. Among them are Moses, Esther, Daniel, Hannah, Ezra, Jehoshaphat, Elijah, Joseph, Solomon, Peter and Paul. The gospels tell us that Jesus fasted for forty days and forty nights after his baptism, in preparation for his public ministry.

Jesus teaches us not to be showy about our fasting (or praying, or giving). If our purpose becomes demonstrating our religiosity, we have missed the point. Jesus says to wash your face so that people can't tell. This is between you and God.

If you want to give this kind of fasting a try, consider giving something up for a time. The goal is to draw closer to God. If you give up lunch, use the time for prayer. If you give up coffee, consider taking the money you would have spent and giving it to alleviate world hunger. With your doctor's permission try a juice-only fast. See what happens. I guarantee you, something will.

14

Almsgiving (Generosity)

Do not store up for yourselves treasures on earth, where moth and rust consume and where thieves break in and steal; but store up for yourselves treasures in heaven, where neither moth nor rust consumes and where thieves do not break in and steal. For where your treasure is, there your heart will be also.

—Matthew 6:19-21

"Where your treasure is, there will your heart be also," Jesus says in this passage from the Sermon on the Mount. He doesn't say, "Where your heart is, your treasure will inevitably follow." He implies that where you put your money, your heart will inevitably follow. One might even conclude that where we invest our money, our heart, our inward focus, our passion, our life, will be.

Your god is that which you love the most, that in which you trust and believe with all your heart. The church reformer Martin Luther taught in his Large Catechism that your god is that from which you expect all good and that to which you turn in times of distress. In what do you believe with all your heart? In what do you trust for fulfillment in life? One way to find out is to look at your checkbook and your appointment book. We may claim one God, but in fact, we are constantly worshipping a pantheon of gods. How we spend our treasures of time and money may be the best indicator of what we actually believe in.

Jesus was once cornered and asked which was the greatest commandment. His response was the *Shema*: Love the Lord your God with all your heart, soul, mind and strength. This is the first and greatest commandment. The second, he said, was like it: Love your neighbor as yourself.

Could it be that if we want to direct our heart toward God, one way is by directing our financial resources in that direction? Giving is a form of prayer: something that directs us toward God. This is why there is an offering at every worship service. Giving is an act of worship. Generosity is a Christian faith practice.

How would one direct ones resources toward God? One cannot read the Bible without encountering God's concern about worship, prayer, righteousness, the poor, the widow, the orphan or the sojourner (alien, stranger, wanderer). In the Parable of the Sheep and the Goats, Matthew 25, Jesus says, "I was hungry and you gave me food, I was thirsty and you gave me something to drink, I was a stranger and you welcomed me, I was naked and you gave me clothing, I was sick and you took care of me, I was in prison and you visited me."

1 John 3:17 says, "How does God's love abide in anyone who has the world's goods and sees a brother or sister in need and yet refuses help?" God's love abides in us as we share our treasure with the world in need.

In your prayers today, take stock of your own generosity. How much of what you earn is given away? The Hebrew Bible set a standard of 10%, called a tithe. Jesus suggested a heart turned toward God might go even farther, like Zaccheus' 50% or the widow giving 100% - everything she had. Pray with your checkbook today. If it's tax season, it's time to take stock of your giving anyway. How much did you give? How much would you like to give? To what would you like to give? Where is your heart? As you take time for silence, where do you sense God's heart is?

Use this time to pray about your giving. Make some decisions. What are you going to give this year? To whom? Make a commitment, in conversation with your family. Write down your commitment and share it with the organizations or people to whom you wish to give.

Make giving a priority, for where your treasure is, there will your heart be also.

15

Making time

*He said to them, "Come away to a deserted place all by yourselves
and rest a while." For many were coming and going,
and they had no leisure even to eat.
And they went away in the boat to a deserted place by themselves.
Now many saw them going and recognized them, and they hurried
there on foot from all the towns and arrived ahead of them.*

—Mark 6:31-33

By now, if you've been trying some of these prayer methods, you have probably noticed that it takes time. For most of us, if we don't set aside time in our schedule for prayer, the rest of life will come crashing in and crowd out our spiritual time. Physical needs tend to crowd out spiritual needs. Like our finances, our time is part of the treasure that directs our heart. How we spend our time says something about our priorities. Any relationship takes an investment of time. This is also true of our relationship with God.

The gospels describe Jesus as having a very active ministry. He was a busy guy. His ministry of preaching, teaching and healing had become so popular in a world without hospitals as we know them, that they were being mobbed. Mark 6 says they were so busy they didn't have time to eat. But Jesus knew they wouldn't be able to keep it up without time for prayer and reflection, so he encouraged them to come away to a deserted place and rest.

I prefer to pray in the morning. My mind is fresh, and not so many people are usually pressing demands on me early in the morning. Some prefer to pray at noon. Others in the evening. It doesn't really matter. In the perfect world, we would make sure to pray all of those times. What's important is to find a time that works for you. It needs to be a realistic time you will actually use. It also needs to be a time when you can pray uninterrupted. This is why I like to walk. I'm hard to track down.

In another passage, Mark 1:35-37, Jesus gets up early by himself to pray:

> *In the morning, while it was still very dark, he got up and went out to a deserted place, and there he prayed. And Simon and his companions hunted for him. When they found him, they said to him, "Everyone is searching for you."*

Today, take time to pray about when to pray. That may sound amusing, but it's an important thing to pray about. First, if you use a calendar, pull it out and read through it. Pray over your time priorities. Resist the urge to reorganize your entire calendar for the moment. If urgent things come to mind, write them down in your prayer journal and come back to them later. What do your time allocations say about your priorities?

Then think about when you will pray. What time will actually work for prayer in your life? Try a few different times and see what works for you. Set aside 15 minutes at first, but know that as you progress, you will find yourself wanting more time, first a half hour, later an hour. Try different times. Find one that fits like a glove. If you use a calendar a lot, write your prayer times into your calendar for the next few months. You will be more likely to take the time if you have budgeted for it. Writing it down will help you keep first things first.

16

Walking

While they were talking and discussing, Jesus himself came near and went with them, but their eyes were kept from recognizing him.

—Luke 24:15-16

So far I've mentioned both walking and sitting in prayer. I'm not sure where we get the idea that we have to be stationary while praying. There is a long history in the church of praying while walking. If your house is full, getting out of the house can be a way to find uninterrupted time.

Certainly, sitting is more conducive to using a prayer journal. It's hard to write in a book while walking. I have been known, however, to make notes in my phone while walking. I keep a prayer list on my phone, so I often have it out to order my prayer time. Sometimes, however, it is better to leave the book and the phone behind, to walk and pray. If your goal is contemplation, where you are a passive recipient in prayer, offering nothing, then leave everything behind.

In Luke's gospel, a couple of people are walking down the road, grieving the crucifixion of Jesus of Nazareth, when the resurrected Christ walks alongside them. They do not recognize him. Often in life, Jesus is walking alongside us, but we are too distracted to recognize it. Today, we will practice attentiveness.

For today's prayer exercise, take a walk with Jesus. Begin with giving thanks for all the good gifts God has given you in your life.

Remember those in need. Pray for your neighborhood. Rehearse the first Bible passage that pops into your head. Then just leave time to breathe in the air and listen for God's voice.

When you return, write a sentence or two in your prayer journal. How did walking work for you? What promptings of the Spirit emerged as you prayed?

Even if this did not rock your world, try it again in a day or two. It may take a while to grow on you. It's a good tool to have in your prayer toolbox.

One last comment about walking. You don't need to go far. Many churches and retreat centers have labyrinths. A labyrinth is usually a round walking path about the size of a driveway, that looks like a maze. It is not a maze. A maze has a complex set of optional paths, some of which lead to dead ends. The goal is to find your way. A labyrinth has a single, winding path to the center, and then out.

Find a labyrinth near you and try it out. A metaphor for the journey of life, this simple walking path comes with unexpected turns. Follow it to the center. Pray for yourself and your family on the way in. Pray for others on your way out. Or use any of the prayer exercises in this book. There is no right or wrong way to pray the labyrinth. It is just a way to slow you down and create a meditative environment.

17

Music

Do not get drunk with wine, for that is debauchery; but be filled with the Spirit, as you sing psalms and hymns and spiritual songs among yourselves, singing and making melody to the Lord in your hearts, giving thanks to God the Father at all times and for everything in the name of our Lord Jesus Christ.

—Ephesians 5:18-20

The text actually reads something like this in the original language: "Do not be drunk with wine… but be drunk with the Spirit." The writer of Ephesians invites us to have our spirits lifted by the Spirit, making music in our hearts, singing songs. This is not the first time being filled with the Spirit and being drunk are related. In Acts 2, as the disciples are filled with the Spirit on Pentecost, those standing nearby seem to think they are drunk. Peter even has to begin his Pentecostal sermon with the words, "These people are not drunk, as you suppose." I have never had to begin a sermon with these words.

For most of us, there are few things that lift our spirits to a euphoric state as much as music. It is no surprise to me that music has been a part of worship since the beginning of human civilization. Next to theology, Luther considered no other art to be equal to music, which quiets and cheers the human soul, therefore driving away the devil, the originator of depressing worries and troubled thoughts.

In Luther's day, if one did not play an instrument or sing, one would have to go to concerts, to church or to the tavern to experience music. These days, we have music on our phones, our iPods, our stereos, our televisions and in our cars. I can't imagine a time in history when such a wide variety of music was so immediately accessible.

Music lifts the soul. Some music can have the opposite effect. Some music gives voice to lament and sorrow. There is music for every season of life.

Have you ever had the experience of going on a long drive by yourself and listening to music for a couple of hours? How did it affect your spirit? Many people, though not all, find this to be a meditative way to calm your spirit.

For today's prayer exercise, try a little music. If you are a musician, pull out your guitar or sit at your piano and play for 30 minutes. Don't learn new music, just play what comes to mind. If you're not musically inclined, get in your car and sing with the radio, or go for a walk with your ear buds. Choose you music carefully. Create a playlist that celebrates life and calls us to a higher purpose.

When you have listened for a while, turn off the music and enjoy a time of silence. What music is stuck in your head? What insights does your state of mind bring to the surface? Consider writing some reflections in your prayer journal.

18

Journaling

I, John, your brother who share with you in Jesus the persecution and the kingdom and the patient endurance, was on the island called Patmos because of the word of God and the testimony of Jesus. I was in the spirit on the Lord's day, and I heard behind me a loud voice like a trumpet saying, "Write in a book what you see and send it to the seven churches, to Ephesus, to Smyrna, to Pergamum, to Thyatira, to Sardis, to Philadelphia, and to Laodicea."

—Revelation 1:9-11

In exile on the island of Patmos, John has a lot of time for prayer and reflection. He describes being "in the Spirit" on the Lord's day (Sunday). Perhaps he was in worship. Perhaps not. In any case, he has a mystical experience. Deep in prayer, he has a vision and hears a voice like a trumpet telling him to write down what he sees and send it to each of seven churches.

The Bible says faith comes by hearing, but if the Bible is any indication, it also leads to writing. There are four gospels in our Bible, and a couple dozen more that aren't. The apostle Paul wrote letters to churches. Christians throughout the centuries have written sermons, tracts and devotional materials as I am right now.

I have already mentioned journaling as tool for other prayer exercises. Today let's consider it head on. For years I was encouraged by spiritual leaders to journal. I tried on and off for decades. Inevitably, I would start, go a few days and then stop. It just didn't work for me. Then, many years later, I was stuck in my prayer life. I listened to a podcast that once again suggested journaling. It simply said to write a couple of sentences each day. Begin with the word, "Yesterday…"

The time was right. This worked for me. Instead of hand-writing a journal, I opened my laptop each morning and began, "Yesterday…" Inevitably, the first thing that came to mind was some conflict I had had, or something I regretted saying. Intending to only write a couple of sentences, I would pour out my heart. I would confess my sins. I would think through how to right wrongs. I would consider how to handle difficult personalities. I would hear God tugging at my heart.

I found myself using the journal to collect poetry, Scriptures and ideas that had moved me. I'd write down things people had said that caught my attention. I wrote down dreams that I had as soon as I woke up. Our dreams tell us much if we listen and pay attention. I would write down goals, hopes, dreams and visions. Many sermons were brainstormed here.

After a few months I looked back over what I had written and could see how my thoughts had evolved. I would be in prayer about a situation, and would recall something similar that had happened. I looked back and could see patterns in the way I handled things, the way I screwed things up, and in the way the congregation I served tended to function. It became a source of insight.

If you've been resisting journaling to this point, give in. Give it a try. You may find it is the key to unlocking your prayer life. Even if it doesn't work, as it didn't for me for decades, you may find it to be just the right tool years down the road. Add this to your toolbox. Begin today, with the word, "Yesterday…"

19

Confession

Create in me a clean heart, O God,
and put a new and right spirit within me.
Do not cast me away from your presence,
and do not take your holy spirit from me.
Restore to me the joy of your salvation,
and sustain in me a willing spirit.

—Psalm 51:10-12

Confession is good for the soul. The Roman Catholic Church has a strong tradition of private confession with a priest. In John's first letter he says we are deceiving ourselves if we say we have no sin. There is no truth in that. We all know it.

One my favorite sermon illustrations is of a boy at his grandmother's house. Throwing stones into the pond behind her house, he saw grandma's goose and started throwing stones at it. One hit its mark and killed the goose on the spot. He quickly grabbed a shovel and buried the goose in the woods. Later, his sister whispered, "I saw what you did." Long story short, he agreed to do her chores until further notice, in exchange for her silence. After days of washing dishes and other chores, he finally decided to go to his grandmother and tell her the truth. Once he finished, she said, "I know. I saw the whole thing from my kitchen window. I was just wondering how long you were going to go on in slavery."

Sin leaves us in bondage. Confession frees us from slavery.

Confessing to others is a good thing. Before we do that we have to be ready to confess to ourselves and to God. For today's exercise, take a personal moral inventory. Be prepared. This isn't easy. Where have you dropped the ball? Who have you betrayed? When have you hurt others, defied God, participated in self-destructive or other-destructive behavior? How has greed called the shots in your life? What do you need to get off your chest? Write everything that comes to mind. Leave space to brainstorm a response later. This is your private journal. No one needs to see it.

Next, go back through what you have written and write next to each item some things you could do about it. If something is particularly troubling, make a commitment to go talk to someone about it: a counselor, therapist or pastor. If there is someone with whom you need to make amends, do it. Pray for each person on your list. Know that God forgives sin. Sometimes we need to hear that word of forgiveness. The person you hurt may or may not be prepared to forgive. Even if they do, there may be permanent scars, and consequences that don't go away. If we say we have no sin, we deceive ourselves. You may hear a word of forgiveness in church, or privately from your pastor. Once you have heard that word of forgiveness, return to your journal and cross out that line.

Here is where liturgical rites can be healing. Some churches have a confession every week. Some days are set aside for confession and absolution, like Ash Wednesday and Maundy Thursday. I have seen rites in which people write things down on paper, and then bring them to a brazier (barbecue) and burn them. Amazon sells dissolving paper. These can be brought to a baptismal font where people can see their sins melt away in the waters of baptism. Other churches invite people to nail their sins to the cross as a sign of forgiveness.

If today doesn't feel like the right day to tackle this big topic, skip to the next chapter and come back to this one when you are ready. Confession is only possible when we are convinced that we are forgiven by a God who loves us with an everlasting and invincible love.

20

Table Prayer

*When he was at the table with them, he took bread,
blessed and broke it, and gave it to them.*

—Luke 24:30

If I were to guess, I would imagine that the place most prayers get said in homes is at the table. If a family prays no other time together, they will often pray at the table. Perhaps it is that breaking bread is itself a sacred act. We give thanks for our daily bread, as Jesus taught us in his prayer.

For today's exercise, pray at each meal, whether at the table or over the sink, whether at home or out to eat. Pray at every meal. If this is already your pattern, then take today to learn a new table prayer. Here are some common table prayers.

> *Come Lord Jesus, be our guest, and let these gifts to us be blessed. Amen.*

> *God is great. God is good. Let us thank God for our food. By God's hands we all are fed. Give us now our daily bread.*

> *Lord God, heavenly Father, bless us and these Thy gifts which we are about to receive from Thy bountiful goodness, through Jesus Christ our Lord. Amen.*

> *Bless O Lord, this food to our use, and us to Thy loving service;*
> *And make us ever mindful of the needs of others, for Jesus'*

sake. Amen.

Dear Lord, bless this food to the nourishment of our bodies and us to thy service. In Christ's name we pray, Amen.

There are many more prayers that can be found in prayer books, hymnals and online. These prayers go by fairly quickly. They are a quick word of thanks, but they don't foster a state of focused prayer. Consider a couple of possibilities to deepen your table prayer.

After the prayer, while people are eating, read a Scripture passage and discuss it. There are many devotional books for this purpose, like *Christ in Our Home, Home Altar* and others.

Consider praying at the end of the meal. During the meal ask your family who in their lives is in need of prayer. You will be surprised how this deepens the conversation. Difficult teachers, suicidal friends, families going through divorce, and more will come up. At the end of the meal before everyone gets up, take turns praying for the people who have been mentioned. Then don't forget to have everyone chip in with the dishes.

In your journal write down how this discipline of mealtime prayer has affected you.

21

Praying for the World

And he said to them, "Go into all the world
and proclaim the good news to the whole creation.

—Mark 16:15

There are several really fun ways to pray for the world. Perhaps there are some places that are near and dear to your heart. We adopted our daughter from an orphanage in Russia, so that part of the world is always in our hearts. Our synod (a group of congregations that work together) have a companion relationship with the church in Peru and the church in the Central African Republic. We pray for them frequently. Perhaps you have friends or relatives in another country.

For today's prayer exercise, write in your journal a list of all the people you know who live in another country. Then list the countries with which are in a state of war. List any countries you plan to visit. List countries that have had tragedies or been in the news recently. When you have finished run down your list, and pray for each country by name, and any people you know there.

Another way to pray for the world is to hold a globe or a world map in your hands. We'll talk more about praying with children later, but one fun thing to do is to spin the globe and then have the child put down their finger until it stops. On which country did it land? What do you know about that country and its people? Look some things up, and then remember them in prayer.

In groups and in worship I have seen leaders lay out a world map on the floor or a table, the size of a tablecloth. Then people are invited to come and place polished stones or lighted votive candles on a country or several countries of their choosing. Try using the puzzle prayer mentioned in the next chapter, with the name of a different country on each puzzle piece.

If there is a country for which you see yourself praying on a regular basis, set up a decorative table with a candle and several items from the country in your home, or hang a piece of artwork from that country on your wall. Each time you pass by, remember that country in prayer.

One final thought. There is a soulful litany that names all the countries of the world in song. Consider using *For the Healing of the Nations* in your worship. The text is by Susan Briehl. Music is by John D. Becker. It comes from *Litany of the Saints,* Augsburg Fortress, 2009.

22

Praying with Kids – Puzzles, Clay, Candles

At that time the disciples came to Jesus and asked, 'Who is the greatest in the kingdom of heaven?' He called a child, whom he put among them, and said, 'Truly I tell you, unless you change and become like children, you will never enter the kingdom of heaven. Whoever becomes humble like this child is the greatest in the kingdom of heaven.

—Matthew 18:1-4

Jesus used children as a role model for faith. If we see faith as trusting God, rather than believing doctrines or creeds, then children have more faith than adults. They tend to trust God, because they have to. Spending time with children is good for your spiritual life.

The next few ideas are for praying with children, but one could say they are for adults who also want to pray creatively and playfully. Try some of these to stir your imagination. The spiritual life of children comes alive through play. We have a playful God. Roll with it.

Try this tactile exercise, then save it for a future opportunity with prayer stations (continue below). Find a small jigsaw puzzle in your closet, or purchase an inexpensive one of 16-24 pieces. Spray paint the puzzle pieces white. Then, on each piece write a prayer concern. You could write a country on each piece. You could write concerns, like hunger, poverty, famine... You could write people in your life for whom you pray, family members, national, state and local leaders and the like. Another option is to put spiritual values on the pieces, like the nine fruits of the Spirit in Galatians 5:22: love, joy, peace, patience, kindness… Complete it with prayer, giving, honesty and other values you want to instill.

Then assemble the puzzle with your child. As they hold each piece in their hand, looking for its place, invite them to pray for that concern. This can also make a great exercise to pull from your bag of tricks for an active child in worship.

This is not just for children. I recently spent 15 minutes with a puzzle like this and found myself very centered and focused in the exercise.

Another exercise is to get some modeling clay, or play dough. As you pray with children about people, situations or countries, invite the child to make things. Keep the "sculptures" on the kitchen table for the week as a reminder of that prayer.

One last idea for today would be lighting a candle for someone. Often lighting a candle is a signal that something sacred is happening. Home is church too. When you sit down to pray, light a candle for your child or for yourself. If the child is old enough, let him or her light the candle, then pray a prayer together, perhaps one that you are encouraging your child to read.

23

Praying with Kids:
Blessing, Coloring, Sidewalk
Chalk, and Post-it Note Prayers

Then little children were being brought to him in order that
he might lay his hands on them and pray. The disciples spoke
sternly to those who brought them; but Jesus said,
'Let the little children come to me, and do not stop them;
for it is to such as these that the kingdom of heaven belongs.'
And he laid his hands on them and went on his way.

—Matthew 19:13-15

Children are a blessing. They see the world through eyes of wonder
as we once did. Use your prayer time with children not only to grow
their faith life, but also to renew yours. If you don't have kids of
your own, then borrow some. Volunteer at your church. Take time to
do whatever training and background check is required. It will be a
blessing to you. If you're not good with kids, offer to help someone
who is.

Bless the children. Jesus prayed for children. Consider offering a
blessing to children in worship, Sunday school or children's
activities. Under the supervision of the pastor or the appropriate staff
person, invite children to share something for which they are
thankful, and someone or something for which they would like to
pray. Don't let it throw you if they pray for a toy. Children aren't
encumbered by the same restrictions we adults are. Mark the sign of
the cross on the child's forehead and offer a prayer for that concern.

Color with children. Get a coloring book of nature scenes or Bible scenes. Many things can be downloaded from the internet these days. Pull out some good old-fashioned crayons and color with the child. Talk about the story above in the form of *Lectio Divina*. What's going on in this story? Who are you in the story? Or color with blank sheets of drawing paper. Ask the child to draw and color some things for which they are thankful. You do the same.

Purchase some sidewalk chalk from the store. At your home or church, draw on the sidewalk or driveway prayer concerns or things for which you are thankful, like you did with the coloring exercise.

Finally, consider writing prayer concerns on Post-it notes. Place the Post-it notes in different places around the house to remind people to pray. For example, when remembering those who are hungry in the world, place the note on the refrigerator.

Once again, these prayers are not just for children. Many people are kinesthetic learners. They experience the world in a tactile way. Hands-on prayer can be very meaningful for those folks, and even for those who are visual or auditory learners.

24

Prayer Stations

Keep these words that I am commanding you today in your heart.
Recite them to your children and talk about them when you
are at home and when you are away, when you lie down
and when you rise. Bind them as a sign on your hand, fix them
as an emblem on your forehead, and write them on the doorposts
of your house and on your gates.

—Deuteronomy 6:6-9

Recite the commandments to your children and talk about them when you are home and when you are away. Home and away. That pretty much covers the gamut. When you lie down and when you rise. Bind them to your hand and forehead and write them on the doorpost of your house and on your gates. I think the idea here is to surround yourself with reminders.

Take some of the ideas mentioned in the last few sections and put them together and you have prayer stations. These can be done at home, in a small group Bible study or in a worship service. At a few tables around the room (or around the house), have some items set up, like the map previously mentioned with polished stones, clay, the puzzle.

For adults, one station could have a little bit of incense and cards with prayers on them to be prayed. In worship, one station could be a place where someone will pray with you and for you. One station could be an anointing with oil on the forehead for healing. These lend themselves well to worship.

There are an unlimited number of possibilities to invite people into prayer creatively. One website with a large collection of ideas is by Theresa Cho: http://theresaecho.com/interactive-prayer-stations.

If you are praying at home alone, or as a family, set up a prayer station in all the rooms of your home. Start with a few rooms and see how it evolves. One room might simply be an icon on the wall, or a cross. Another room might have a table with some items from a country that you pray for regularly. Another room may have family photos of people for whom you pray regularly. Remember that setting up these stations is prayer as well.

Make your home a Hall of Prayer.

25

The Lord's Prayer

Pray then in this way:
Our Father in heaven, hallowed be your name.
Your kingdom come. Your will be done, on earth as it is in heaven.
Give us this day our daily bread. And forgive us our debts, as we
also have forgiven our debtors. And do not bring us to the time of
trial, but rescue us from the evil one.

—Matthew 6:9-13

When Jesus taught his disciples to pray he taught a short and simple prayer. Unlike many prayers you might come across, this one is pretty short. It can be prayed slowly in less than 30 seconds. In fact, Jesus warns his disciples not to pray like others who "think they will be heard for their many words." Words can be limiting.

Many people pray this prayer once or twice a day: in the morning and in the evening before bed. It is easy to take it for granted, rattling through the words without thinking about what they mean.

For today's exercise, pray the Lord's Prayer slowly, considering each petition. The Small Catechism divides the Lord's Prayer into seven petitions, with an introduction and a doxology. Pray each petition, one at a time and consider the question afterwards. If you're walking, ponder the questions. If you're sitting, consider writing in your prayer journal.

Introduction: Our Father, who art in heaven

What was your relationship with your father like? What does it mean to you to think of God as a loving father who has all of your best interests in mind?

First Petition: Hallowed be Thy name.

How do you honor God's name and keep it holy? In what ways do we take God's name in vain, making it cheap?

Second Petition: Thy kingdom come.

The kingdom of God refers to the fulfillment of God's reign as described in the Bible, where the hungry are fed, the naked are clothed, all are welcome, death is destroyed and every tear is wiped from our eyes. Where do you see God's kingdom breaking into our world? How might you be a part of that?

Third Petition: Thy will be done, on earth as it is in heaven.

Where is God's will not being done? How is God calling you to speak and act prophetically in those situations?

Fourth Petition: Give us this day our daily bread.

Give thanks for all that you have, and ask for what you need.

Fifth Petition: And forgive us our trespasses, as we forgive those who trespass against us.

This is a dangerous prayer. We are asking God to forgive us in the same way that we forgive others. Where have you erred this week? From whom do you need forgiveness? Who do you need to forgive?

Sixth Petition: And lead us not into temptation

Where are you being tempted right now? In which situations do you need to be careful, and pray for strength?

Seventh Petition: But deliver us from evil.

Where is there evil in the world? For whom do you need to pray? Where might you be called to intervene?

Doxology: For Thine is the kingdom, and the power and the glory, forever and ever. Amen.

Take this opportunity to give thanks to God for creation and the mystery of life.

When you are finished, go back and say the Lord's Prayer from start to finish, straight through. Has praying it slowly and thoughtfully helped you focus more clearly on what is being said?

26

Dreaming

For God speaks in one way, and in two, though people do not perceive it. In a dream, in a vision of the night, when deep sleep falls on mortals, while they slumber on their beds…

—Job 33:14-15

Some people remember their dreams, and others do not. A 1998 study by Stepansky showed that about 1/3 of people say they dream 10 or more times a month. Another third, 1 to 9 times a month. The rest claim to dream once a month or not at all. Scientists believe that all people dream, but some don't tend to remember their dreams, unless they are awakened in the middle of the night.

God speaks through dreams. Even if a dream is not vivid, many people have experienced going to bed with a troubling problem, and waking up with a solution. A list of those who have dreams and visions (wakeful dreams) in the Bible is like a biblical who's who. Abraham, Jacob, Joseph, Pharaoh, Pharaoh's cupbearer, Samuel, Daniel, Joseph, Pilate's wife, Zechariah, Peter, Paul, John. With a list like this do we dare ignore dreams? Also, if God speaks through dreams, does it not follow that dreams can be a form of prayer?

Following your dreams is like fishing. It takes time and patience. For some it's easy to remember dreams. It's understanding them that's difficult. Others may have trouble remembering any dreams at all.

To attempt to listen for God's voice through dreams today, pray now, and then again just before you go to bed, that God speaks through your dreams tonight. Tell your unconscious mind that you'd like to remember your dreams. You might be surprised. It may take several nights, but most people will experience a dream.

Keep a pad and paper by your bedside, so that if you wake up in the morning or in the middle of the night with a dream on your mind, you can write it down. If you go back to sleep, you are likely to forget important details. Writing is key.

Dreams are not linear. They are rarely clear. They are never logical. Sometimes there are things in a dream that defy words. Capture as much of the feeling and sense of the dream as possible. Tell someone about the dream, to hear their thoughts about it.

Write down your dreams over a period of days or weeks, creating a dream journal, or include them in your prayer journal. Pay special attention to recurring dreams. In time, patterns will emerge. Your dreams may reveal deep-seated fears and insecurities. They may also unveil deeply held convictions, hopes and aspirations. The apostle Paul was in Troas agonizing over where to go next. He had a dream in which a man urged him to come to Macedonia. With that, the gospel entered Europe for the first time.

The question is: What do your dreams say about where you are, and where God is calling you to go? Listen to your dreams. They are a window to your soul, and are one of the ways God may be speaking.

27

Speaking in Tongues

Likewise the Spirit helps us in our weakness;
for we do not know how to pray as we ought,
but that very Spirit intercedes
with sighs too deep for words.

—Romans 8:26

Ecstatic speech is not limited to Christianity. It is known in many religious traditions. Several instances of "tongues" are mentioned in the Bible, though some are significantly different.

In Acts 2, at Pentecost, a group of devout Jewish pilgrims from around the world meet in Jerusalem. They each hear the Galilean disciples speaking in their native language. The miracle is that everyone understands what is being said. It is the reversal of the Tower of Babel story in Genesis.

The apostle Paul discusses tongues. He tells the Corinthian church (chapter 14) to limit it to three people, speaking one at a time, with someone interpreting what is being said. He is concerned for unbelievers encountering chaos. "For those who speak in a tongue do not speak to other people but to God; for nobody understands them, since they are speaking mysteries in the Spirit." In Jerusalem at Pentecost speaking in tongues means everyone understands. In Corinth with Paul, speaking in tongues means no one understands.

Speaking in tongues is a personal experience, though not necessarily private. My personal experiences with speaking in tongues in prayer have come at highly emotional times of crisis. The experience of a

Pentecostal friend of mine is just the opposite. He says he can turn it on and off.

The Romans 8 passage above may broadly encompass the experience of tongues from the quiet prayer in ones closet, to the most ardent Pentecostal. The Spirit helps us in our weakness, with sighs too deep for words.

One thing is for sure, speaking in tongues was a normative experience for the early church. For many Christians today, in particular the rapidly growing community of Pentecostals, praying in tongues is important part of their faith life.

Tongues are a gift of the Spirit. The gift may only come through hours of prayer, or not at all. Paul makes it clear not everyone has this gift. "Are all apostles? Are all prophets? Are all teachers? Do all work miracles? Do all possess gifts of healing? Do all speak in tongues? Do all interpret? But strive for the greater gifts. And I will show you a still more excellent way." (1 Corinthians 12:29-31)

If you want to learn more, consider visiting a Pentecostal Church. Talk to a friend who has experienced this gift of the Spirit. Pray not just with your mind, but with your spirit. Move beyond intellectual exercises. Allow God to carry you in prayer. Allow the Spirit to be the prayer. Ask God for the gift, trusting that God will give you what you need, according to your unique gifts.

28

Praying for Your Enemies

You have heard that it was said, "You shall love your neighbor and hate your enemy." But I say to you, Love your enemies and pray for those who persecute you, so that you may be children of your Father in heaven; for he makes his sun rise on the evil and on the good, and sends rain on the righteous and on the unrighteous.

—Matthew 5:43-45

This is a hard teaching from the Sermon on the Mount. Jesus teaches us to love our enemies. Granted, this does not mean allowing abusers to continue to abuse. It does not mean there are no consequences. Forgiveness does not mean restoration to a position of trust. It means refraining from vengeance, both for your sake and for the sake of your enemy.

Loving those who love you is no great feat. Loving your enemies takes a higher level of spiritual maturity. Praying for your enemies is not for beginners, but I invite you to try it on. If you have been recently abused, you may not be ready yet. Praying for your enemies does not mean pretending the offense did not happen and going back to the way things were. It means relinquishing your right to get even. It means freeing yourself from having to carry around a grudge. It is releasing the past in order to embrace a new tomorrow.

Praying for your enemies might entail praying for their conversion from hatred to love, from brokenness to healing. We pray these prayers even in the midst of unlikely outcomes.

Who are your enemies? Start a list in your prayer journal. Begin far from home to start. Who are the enemies of the state? Who are criminals who have committed crimes against humanity? Write their names down. In the years after the planes hit the Twin Towers, some congregations prayed for Osama bin Laden. People would push back on this, but isn't it precisely what Jesus taught in Matthew 5? How might you pray for those on your list so far? Even if the only prayer you can pray is, "Help them see the error of their ways," this is a start.

Then move to enemies closer to home. Who wishes you ill? Who has hurt you or someone you love in the past? Who do you need to forgive, not necessarily to bring them back into your life, but so you can move past the hurt? Write the names, as difficult as it may be.

You do not need to pray for all these enemies daily, but if we are to be faithful to Jesus' teaching in the Sermon on the Mount, we must, from time to time, pray for our enemies, both in our personal prayers, and in the prayers of the whole church assembled in worship. This takes courage and faith.

The apostle Paul echoed Jesus' words in his letter to the church in Rome. He even suggested we feed our enemies if they are hungry. Give them something to drink if they are thirsty. It is taking the higher road. If you're having trouble praying for your enemies, read this passage from time to time:

Do not repay anyone evil for evil, but take thought for what is noble in the sight of all. If it is possible, so far as it depends on you, live peaceably with all. Beloved, never avenge yourselves, but leave room for the wrath of God; for it is written, 'Vengeance is mine, I will repay, says the Lord.' No, 'if your enemies are hungry, feed them; if they are thirsty, give them something to drink; for by doing this you will heap burning coals on their heads.' Do not be overcome by evil, but overcome evil with good.
—Romans 12:17-21

29

Answered Prayer

*Isaac prayed to the Lord for his wife, because she was barren; and
the Lord granted his prayer, and his wife Rebekah conceived.*

—Genesis 25:21

Jesus said in the Sermon on the Mount, "Ask and you shall receive.
Seek and you shall find. Knock and the door shall be opened to
you." (Matthew 7:7) God loves you and wants the best for you. I
believe Jesus is pointing to an often misunderstood truth: What you
set as the desire of your heart, you may just receive. This cuts both
ways. If you really want to be rich, and you are willing to sacrifice
everything else in life for it, you might just get there. But Jesus
warns, "What does it profit you if you gain the whole world, but lose
your soul?" (Luke 9:25) Be careful what you ask for.

God wants to give you good gifts: daily bread, love, hope, joy. It is
God's desire that all have enough. If you seek these things, in most
cases you will likely find them. Where sin has marred human
community, things will be more difficult.

Along with this promise is the encouragement to ask for the desire of
our hearts. What I asked for at the age of seven is different than what
I ask for today, but that's okay. Ask. Seek. Knock. Keep asking.
Keep seeking. Keep knocking.

For today's prayer exercise, make a list of some of the things you
desire with all your heart. What are the biggies? If you could ask for
only a few things, what would be on your list? Write it down.

When you have finished writing, read down through your list slowly and make it a petition.

Then consider what you are doing to realize these hopes and dreams. It is somewhat disingenuous to ask God for something, and then not lift a finger ourselves. It would be like a farmer praying God grant a bountiful harvest, but not being willing to plant, weed or reap.

The more you pray this prayer, you may find God transforming your priorities. Daily prayer has a focusing effect. As you grow, the desires of your heart grow too. As you pray, you will find God will sanctify your prayers. As you spend time with God, read Scripture and pray, your desires will little by little come into line with God's desires.

30

Unanswered Prayer

My God, my God, why have you forsaken me?

—Matthew 27:46

God answers prayer, most of the time. There are many spiritual leaders and mystics who have, over the years, felt the silence of God. We cannot talk about the voice of God without acknowledging the silence of God. We cannot talk about the presence of God without talking about the absence of God. We cannot talk about the revealed God without acknowledging the hidden God who requires revealing.

Even Jesus experienced the absence of God. Only Matthew's gospel has the courage to record this cry of Jesus in the throes of death: "My God, my God, why have you forsaken me?" Even Jesus felt abandoned by God. This is a quote from Psalm 22. Psalm 22 includes, "My God, my God, why have you forsaken me?" Then Psalm 23 says, "The Lord is my shepherd, I shall not want." Both sentiments are part of the human experience. The psalms are honest about life and death issues.

Most often we receive answers to our prayers. Eventually, things go one way or the other. But sometimes, there seems to be no answer. Some have suggested there always is an answer, but at times we just can't hear it. That may be true, but even Mother Teresa said she felt God go silent for many years, as if someone turned off a loudspeaker.

For today's prayer exercise, write a list of unanswered prayers. These are not prayers where the answer was "no." These are prayers for which we have received no answer whatsoever. What clarity have you sought, but not received? For most of us, this list will be short. Most of our prayers have been answered, even if it is not the answer we like. (See the next chapter.) Perhaps your list is longer. Give it a go.

As you look over this list of unanswered prayers you have created, ask why there has been no answer? Be honest in your prayers. "Why do we call to you O God, and you do not listen?" Ask God again for an answer. Be willing to commit to some time for listening in silence. How can we expect answers if we will not listen?

Listen also to loved ones and trusted confidants around you. Sometimes God speaks to us through the voices of those around us. It may well be that the answer is right in front of us, but we haven't seen it. Or, it may be that the answer is one we don't like, and therefore we really don't even want to hear it. This is the subject of our next chapter.

31

Not the Answer I Wanted

Father, if you are willing, remove this cup from me;
yet, not my will but yours be done.

—Luke 22:42

Sometimes the answer is "No."

Even Jesus was told, "No." In the Garden of Gethsemane Jesus poured out his heart. One gospel says he was so distraught he sweat blood. As they came to arrest and execute him he prayed, "Father, let this cup pass from me." The "cup" was Jesus' destiny, his crucifixion. His life and ministry had led to this most difficult hour. He didn't want to go through with it, but the die had been cast. He had crossed the Rubicon. Jesus himself had prayed for a way out, and none was given.

Earlier, in the chapter on *tentatio* we talked about Paul's thorn in the flesh. He asked God to take it away. Again the answer was, "No." He was told, "My grace is sufficient for you, for my power is made perfect in weakness." Even the most faithful, Jesus and Paul among them, do not get everything they want. We most likely won't either.

In the last chapter we heard Jesus say, "Ask and you shall receive. Seek and you shall find. Knock and the door shall be opened to you." Jesus taught that God is like a loving parent who wants the very best for us. I want the very best for my children, but that does not mean I give them everything they want. And, giving them their freedom means they will make bad choices, and in a big world, possibly end up in harm's way.

For your prayer exercise today, consider the times that you have wanted something very badly and not gotten your way. Consider the prayers you've offered up for which the answer seemed to be, "No." Write them in your journal or make a mental note.

If you're like most people, some of those situations were huge disappointments. I'm willing to bet, however, that there are some of those situations that you look back upon and think, *Thank God I didn't get what I wanted. It would have been disastrous.* Perhaps you were fired from a job. You felt devastated, but went on to something that you love more than the job you had before. Perhaps you call to mind the love of your life that broke your heart, and realize now it would have been a wreck. A loving parent never gives a child everything.

Some things are truly devastating. There are those who suffer unimaginable tragedy. We believe that God can bring about good from every disaster. This is not to say God causes every disaster. It is simply to trust that God can bring good out of every evil. It is to say that we believe in the God of the resurrection, who has conquered death. This is what the cross is all about. It is why we call the day Jesus died "Good Friday."

32

Hypocritical prayer

And whenever you pray, do not be like the hypocrites;
for they love to stand and pray in the synagogues and at
the street corners, so that they may be seen by others.
Truly I tell you, they have received their reward.

—Matthew 6:5

Jesus calls a spade a spade. If you've been around public prayer much, you've heard it before: a prayer that seems more designed to impress those in the room than a heartfelt outpouring to God. Sometimes prayer can be a kind of spiritual one-upmanship. If you are praying to be holier than thou, if you are praying to show off your sense of self-righteousness, your heart is not in the right place. Jesus warns us to be vigilant against this kind of showiness. This is one form of hypocrisy. There are others.

Hypocrisy is saying one thing but doing another. If we pray for one thing, but work very hard to accomplish the opposite, that is hypocrisy. It may even be evil. To pray for the world, and then commit violence is the negation of the prayer we prayed. In Isaiah 1:15 God says, "When you stretch out your hands, I will hide my eyes from you; even though you make many prayers, I will not listen; your hands are full of blood." It may be that some prayers are not answered because we didn't really mean them in the first place?

Even praying for something, but not being willing to do anything to make it happen is a form of hypocrisy. It is praying one thing, but doing another. If we pray for an end to hunger, but do not work for it, what does that say about the authenticity of our prayers? If in church or at home we pray for peace, but then go out and stir up conflict, where is the integrity in that?

God's kingdom will come and God's will be done, even without your efforts, or mine. But we pray that God will use us to accomplish God's will on earth as it is in heaven. Jesus prays, "Thy kingdom come, Thy will be done on earth as it is in heaven," and then he carries out an exhausting healing ministry in the community. We are called to be doers of the Word, not just hearers. We are invited to be the body of Christ. The church is to be an expression of Jesus' presence in the world.

Perhaps every prayer to God is also a call to action. When we pray for someone who is sick, we are enjoined to go and visit. When we pray for someone who is grieving, we are called to go and weep with those who weep. If your church prays for the sick, decide who will call on this person. If your church prays for the needy, consider how you will respond to that need.

For today's prayer exercise, go back through your prayer journal for the last 27 days and pick out a few prayers. What action is God calling you to take in light of these prayers? If God has placed these things on your heart, what are you going to do about it, so that your prayers have integrity and authenticity?

33

Public Prayer

But whenever you pray, go into your room
and shut the door and pray to your Father who is in secret;
and your Father who sees in secret will reward you.

—Matthew 6:6

Some have interpreted these words to speak against any form of public prayer. Jesus clearly teaches that prayer is private. We should go to our rooms and pray secretly. But Jesus went to the synagogue, so we know he was not against praying publicly. This passage immediately follows the Matthew 6:5, mentioned in the previous chapter. It is a warning against showy forms of prayer, like those who love to stand on the street corners and pray long prayers to show others their righteousness. The danger here is a lack of humility, not praying publicly.

Furthermore, Jesus prayed with his disciples. He taught them to pray, giving them the Lord's Prayer. He asked them to pray with him in the Garden of Gethsemane. "Could you not watch and pray with me one hour?"

Praying in worship is significantly different than praying in private. In my room I may pray for many personal things. When I am with others, I pray for the needs of the church, the world and all who are in need. When we pray in worship we craft our prayers to bring a group of people into the presence of God. Our prayers move outward to the world. These prayers in the Christian community take on a Christ-centered focus. They are addressed to God in the name of Jesus Christ.

Praying in public is another thing still. Our faith community is of a certain tradition. We may have common customs and beliefs. When we pray in public, we may be praying among Christians of other traditions, who hold different views on various topics. Our prayers take on a broader character. We may even be among those who are not of Christian faith. Our goal should not be to use prayer as a hammer to enforce our sectarian beliefs, or to show others that we are right and they are wrong. Our prayers should seek to unite those present in the love of the God who created the heavens and the earth, not divide.

This is not compromise. This is respect. Every day Christians around the world pray this table prayer: "God is great. God is good. Let us thank God for our food. Amen." This prayer never mentions Jesus. This prayer is not Lutheran, Methodist, Episcopal, Presbyterian, Baptist or Catholic. It is a simple prayer of thanks. Some people pray this prayer at home, yet when in a diverse public event, feel they must insert Jesus to make a point.

If you are asked to pray in public, consider praying the Lord's Prayer, or a paraphrase of it. There is no prayer more Christian than the prayer Jesus taught his disciples. It is not the least bit sectarian. Our Father. May your name be holy. May your reign come, your will be done here on earth as in heaven. Give us our daily bread. Forgive us, as we forgive our neighbors. Save us from the time of trial. Deliver us from evil. For the kingdom, the power and the glory are yours. Now and forever. Amen.

As a prayer exercise, imagine that you are asked to pray in church. Write out a prayer you could pray with other Christians. Imagine you are asked to pray at a dinner. Write out a prayer you would use in that context. Finally, imagine that you were asked to pray at community meeting of some sort where people of various religions were present. Write a prayer that you might pray in that context, that conveys your faith in God with authenticity, but does not belittle or cram beliefs down others' throats. Share these prayers with someone. Take time to discuss them.

34

The Prayer that Calls Us

Then the Lord said,
"I have observed the misery of my people who are in Egypt;
I have heard their cry on account of their taskmasters...
So come, I will send you to Pharaoh to bring my people,
the Israelites, out of Egypt." But Moses said to God, "Who am I that
I should go to Pharaoh, and bring the Israelites out of Egypt?"

—Exodus 3:7, 10-11

Perhaps one of the most important prayers we can pray, besides Meister Eckhardt's "Thank you," is the prayer that seeks our calling. Moses hears the call of God in the burning bush. Isaiah hears God's call amid puffs of smoke and incense. Samuel hears God's call in the middle of the night.

We use the word "call" to refer to a deep sense of being drawn into something. For some it is a deep conviction that builds until it cannot be ignored. For others it is a burning desire to do something of significance. For others it is a sense of responsibility to do something that we actually don't want to do at all. Moses asks, "Who am I to go to Pharaoh?" Jeremiah thinks he's too young. Jonah runs the opposite direction, catches a boat, is thrown overboard and swallowed by a large fish. If you have ever run from your calling, you weren't the first to do so.

The Bible witnesses to a God who calls. A friend of mine was so moved by the need for water in Africa he started a company to build wells in Ethiopia and beyond. Sometimes we are so bothered by something we cannot leave it alone. Perhaps that is the Holy Spirit calling.

Today pray about your calling. Okay, you can't just do it today, but you can start today. Here are some questions to get your started: What things have bothered you your entire life? What recurring dreams have you had? What kinds of things have people told you about yourself over the years? What higher purpose has been burning in your soul for some time? What themes in your life keep resurfacing? What is chasing you?

Take time to ponder these questions. Go for a walk. Take some notes. Revisit the questions in days to come. Answer them again without looking at your previous answers. Do this for several days, then look over your lists. Are any things on all your lists? Are any on most of your lists? If this was God's call, what would it mean for you? Talk with a friend about it.

Jesus' spent forty days in the wilderness before his ministry. The apostle Paul went into the desert of Arabia after his conversion before his public ministry. Jesus prayed all night before even selecting his disciples: "Now during those days he went out to the mountain to pray; and he spent the night in prayer to God. And when day came, he called his disciples and chose twelve of them, whom he also named apostles." (Luke 6:12)

Take time to pray about where God is calling you to go. Pray about what God is calling you to do. Pray about who God is calling you to be.

35

The Prayer of Jabez

Jabez called on the God of Israel, saying, "Oh that you would bless me and enlarge my border, and that your hand might be with me, and that you would keep me from hurt and harm!"
And God granted what he asked.

—1 Chronicles 4:10

A few years ago a book came out called *The Prayer of Jabez.* It became very popular. The book was based the passage above, one that few people knew at the time. Jabez is mentioned briefly in 1 Chronicles 4:9-10, and then never again in the Bible. We know almost nothing about him, except he prayed this prayer, that God answered.

Bless me. Enlarge my border.

There is nothing wrong with this prayer. It is a perfectly appropriate road to take, although there are ditches on either side of the road.

The modern day equivalent would be to pray for God to bless your business or your family. This is a perfectly appropriate thing for which to hope and pray.

The danger arises if this prayer becomes our god, the sole desire of our hearts. If my good becomes more important than the greater good, we're on shaky ground. Even the Psalms warn against it. The second half of Psalm 62:10 says, "…if riches increase, do not set your heart on them."

Jesus warns, in Matthew 6:24, "No one can serve two masters; for a slave will either hate the one and love the other, or be devoted to the one and despise the other. You cannot serve God and wealth." And also in Matthew 6:19-21, "Do not store up for yourselves treasures on earth, where moth and rust consume and where thieves break in and steal; but store up for yourselves treasures in heaven, where neither moth nor rust consumes and where thieves do not break in and steal. For where your treasure is, there your heart will be also."

Today, pray for your family. Name them one at a time by name, slowly. Pray for your extended family as well. Ask God's richest blessings on them. Consider making this a daily ritual.

Pray also for your place of work, or the place where you volunteer. Pray for the people with whom you spend your time, one by one, slowly. Ask God's richest blessings on them.

Pray for yourself, that you will do well in your work. Pray for your daily bread. Pray for your health. Give thanks for your body. Pray that God will "expand your territory," whatever that might mean for you.

Don't stop there. Pray for the world. Pray for the hungry. Pray for the sick. Pray for those living under oppression, hatred or violence. Ask God's richest blessings upon them.

And once you've prayed the prayer of Jabez, pray the prayer of Jesus, "Not my will, but Thy will be done."

36

Praying for your Pastor

Pray also for me, so that when I speak, a message may be given to me to make known with boldness the mystery of the gospel.

—Ephesians 6:19

If you belong to a church, or even visit from time to time, that church has a pastor, priest, minister or spiritual leader of some kind. Pastors are charged with the spiritual care of a large group of people. It is incredibly difficult to be available to so many people as much as might be needed. Pastors often gravitate to those who are hurting, grieving, suffering or lost in any way.

Who cares for the pastor? The pastor may have a bishop, but that bishop usually doesn't live in town, can't come by at a moment's notice, and is not present each Sunday to sense that something may be amiss. Pastors need pastoral care as well.

It is hard each day to put your whole heart on the line, to speak of ultimate things, to stand with people in the hospital, at graveside, at baptismal font, at the altar. There is constant pressure to be all things to all people. Pastors talk about worshipping soulfully, but they are often having to tend to the mechanics of worship. Pastors talk about praying, but often get called away at all hours, and struggle to find time to pray themselves. Every good and interesting pastor I have known has struggled with having a vibrant prayer life. We are called to give. Sometimes we give until we have nothing left. Pastors are human like everyone else. Your pastor needs your prayers. Your congregation and its ministry need your prayers as well.

For today's prayers, take time to remember your pastor and the congregation your pastor serves. Give thanks for your pastor. Remember the times your pastor has been there for you. Think of a time the pastor's message hit a nerve. Consider your pastor's gifts. Forgive your pastors for balls dropped, for flaws and for mistakes. Pray that your pastor might have a robust prayer life. Pray that your pastor might preach the gospel with grace and gusto. Pray that the Spirit will work through your pastor in the lives of others. Pray for your pastor's family, the folks who sometimes pay the price for the service your pastor gives.

Pray for your congregation, that it might be a growing, Christ-centered and outwardly-focused congregation passing the faith to the next generation. Pray for your congregation's witness in the community, that Christ might be seen in all they do. Pray for the needy in your community, that the church might encounter Christ by serving them. Pray that others in the community might be drawn to serve the world alongside your church.

Then consider how you might act on these prayers yourself. Write your pastor a note of appreciation. Buy him or her a cup of coffee. Offer a word of affirmation.

37

Stations of the Cross

*Then [Jesus] said to them all, "If any want
to become my followers, let them deny themselves
and take up their cross daily and follow me.*

—Luke 9:23

The Stations of the Cross are an imaginative way to walk the way of the cross with Jesus. This is an appropriate devotional for Good Friday, when we recall the crucifixion of Jesus. There are 14 stations, or stops along the way from Jesus' trial to his burial. Find the Stations of the Cross on Google Images, or better, find them in a local church.

Once you have found the images, begin with the opening prayer below, then look at the images one at a time. This is not an intellectual exercise. This is an opportunity to imagine yourself walking the way of the cross with Jesus. Look carefully at each picture in silence, using your imagination. Read the Scripture passage I have included below if you need something more concrete. Offer a prayer if you wish, then move on to the next picture. If you spend one minute with each picture, it will take you 15 minutes or so. Two minutes with each picture, half an hour.

Opening Prayer

Lord Jesus, help us to be open to your closeness and presence as we begin our journey to Calvary with you. Help us to find in your Passion and Death the strength to take up our cross and follow you.

We adore You, O Christ, and we praise You because by Your holy cross You have redeemed the world.

1st Station: Jesus is condemned to death

All of them deserted him and fled. —Mark 14:50

Jesus, I confess that I too have denied you at times.

2nd Station: Jesus carries his cross

Then [Jesus] said to them all, "If any want to become my followers, let them deny themselves and take up their cross daily and follow me. —Luke 9:23

Jesus, give me faith to carry the cross in times of trial.

3rd Station: Jesus falls the first time

When they heard this, all in the synagogue were filled with rage. They got up, drove him out of the town, and led him to the brow of the hill on which their town was built, so that they might hurl him off the cliff. —Luke 4:28-29

Jesus, watch over me when I fall.

4th Station: Jesus meets his mother

She was pregnant and was crying out in birth pangs, in the agony of giving birth. —Revelation 12:2

Merciful God, we give you thanks for the humility and compassion of Mary.

5th Station: Simon of Cyrene helps Jesus carry the cross

As they led him away, they seized a man, Simon of Cyrene, who was coming from the country, and they laid the cross on him, and made him carry it behind Jesus. —Luke 23:26

Creator God, give me the courage and strength to bear my cross.

6th Station: Veronica wipes the face of Jesus

For now we see in a mirror, dimly, but then we will see face to face. Now I know only in part; then I will know fully, even as I have been fully known. — 1 Corinthians 13:12

Jesus, may I have the courage to seek your face.

7th Station: Jesus falls the second time

If we say that we have no sin, we deceive ourselves, and the truth is not in us. —1 John 1:8

Jesus, grant me grace that I may not fall into sin, nor be overcome with adversity.

8th Station: Jesus meets the women of Jerusalem

Thus says the Lord:
A voice is heard in Ramah, lamentation and bitter weeping. Rachel is weeping for her children; she refuses to be comforted for her children, because they are no more. —Jeremiah 31:15

Creator God, you care for us even as a mother hen gathers her young under her wing. Protect all children everywhere.

9th Station: Jesus falls a third time

After two days he will revive us; on the third day he will raise us up, that we may live before him. —Hosea 6:2

Loving God, thank you for raising Jesus on the third day. May we have a joyful resurrection like his.

10th Station: Jesus' clothes are taken away

And she gave birth to her firstborn son and wrapped him in bands of cloth, and laid him in a manger, because there was no place for them in the inn. —Luke 2:7

Cleansing Spirit, strip away anything that separates me from love of God and neighbor. Then clothe me in righteousness.

11th Station: Jesus is nailed to the cross

But he was wounded for our transgressions, crushed for our iniquities; upon him was the punishment that made us whole, and by his bruises we are healed. —Isaiah 53:5

Creator God, pierce me with love and repentance as I ponder the mystery of the cross.

12th Station: Jesus dies on the cross

When Jesus had received the wine, he said, "It is finished." Then he bowed his head and gave up his spirit. —John 19:30

Lord Jesus Christ, as you gave your life for me, may I give my life for you.

13th Station: The body of Jesus is taken down from the cross

They took the body of Jesus and wrapped it with the spices in linen cloths, according to the burial custom of the Jews. —John 19:40

We give you thanks that all suffering comes to an end. Sustain us in our hour of trial.

14th Station: Jesus is laid in the tomb.

And she gave birth to her firstborn son and wrapped him in bands of cloth, and laid him in a manger, because there was no place for them in the inn.—John 19:40

Heavenly Father, you walk with us from birth to death. On that day when our bodies are laid to rest, come and gather us up into your kingdom, through Jesus Christ, our resurrected Lord.

Our Father, who art in heaven...

For a creative, less traditional alternative Stations of the Cross, go to http://bishopmike.com/2015/01/19/an-alternate-stations-of-the-cross.

38

Sacred Meal

For I received from the Lord what I also handed on to you, that the Lord Jesus on the night when he was betrayed took a loaf of bread, and when he had given thanks, he broke it and said, "This is my body that is for you. Do this in remembrance of me." In the same way he took the cup also, after supper, saying, "This cup is the new covenant in my blood. Do this, as often as you drink it, in remembrance of me."

—1 Corinthians 11:23b-25

Can a meal itself be prayer? For the majority of Christians around the world, who share the Lord's Supper every Sunday, this meal is communion with God. In fact, many Christians call it Holy Communion.

The Sacrament of the Altar, as it is also known, is not a full meal anymore. At one time the bread and cup were shared in the context of a full meal, in remembrance of Jesus, as he had commanded. "Do this, as often as you drink it, in remembrance of me."

We are told in Acts, written by Luke, the author of the third gospel, that the first Christians "broke bread" together frequently. Some interpret this to mean daily. "Day by day, as they spent much time together in the temple, they broke bread at home and ate their food with glad and generous hearts, praising God and having the goodwill of all the people. And day by day the Lord added to their number those who were being saved." (Acts 2:46-47). These early Christians got together often for a sacred meal together.

We are told, "They devoted themselves to the apostles' teaching and fellowship, to the breaking of bread and the prayers." (Acts 2:42) We have here a description of the life of the first Christians. They devoted themselves to the apostles' teaching. We have this in our New Testament. They devoted themselves to fellowship. This word "fellowship" means community. They shared in life together. They devoted themselves to the breaking of bread. This is code for the Lord's Supper. And they devoted themselves to "the prayers." One might say they devoted themselves to prayer. Others read this to mean they followed a regimen of traditional prayers. In any case, they prayed.

This is an inspiring model for the faith community: study of Scripture, living life together, eating together, celebrating the sacred meal, and praying together. This is what Christian community is.

The sacred meal of Holy Communion is a ritual meal that sends us out into the world. By eating the body of Christ, we become the body of Christ. The meal is an echo of Christ's eating with outcasts and sinners, welcoming them. When he came to Jericho, he immediately ate with the sinner everyone despised: Zaccheus. In turn, Zaccheus gave half of his possessions to the poor. When we eat together and Christ is present, anything can happen.

Plan to receive Holy Communion at your next opportunity. Some churches even have midweek communion. As you eat the bread and drink the wine, remember Jesus' eating with tax collectors and sinners. Remember Jesus' Last Supper with his disciples. Remember the early church eating and drinking in his name. Then remember you are what you eat: the body of Christ.

39

Silence, again

Let the same mind be in you that was in Christ Jesus,

who, though he was in the form of God,
did not regard equality with God
as something to be exploited,

but emptied himself,
taking the form of a slave,
being born in human likeness.
And being found in human form,

he humbled himself
and became obedient to the point of death—
even death on a cross.

—Philippians 2:6-8

In these chapters we have covered many different ways to pray. We have covered several approaches to prayer. There are many more ways to pray than these pages contain.

The danger in doing any or all of these things is that we see the activity as the goal, rather than a tool. We can get so caught up in activity - doing this, saying that, writing a list - that we miss the ultimate goal, which is communion with God.

So come back to the silence. All kinds of prayer are designed to carry us into that place where we commune with God. "Be still and know that I am God." Everything we have discussed to this point is designed to bring us to a place of quiet where we can experience the divine. Mother Teresa used to say, "God cannot fill what is already full."

Our lives are too full. They are full of news, full of busyness, full of work, full of entertainment, full of socializing, full of chores. We are a hyperactive society desperately in need of emptying, spirituality, listening, reflection. So many ills of society would be alleviated with just a little contemplation.

Prayer is more about emptying ourselves than anything else. Paul tells us to have the mind of Christ, who did not regard his status, but emptied himself, humbling himself, becoming a servant, giving his life.

Prayer is about where we put our focus. Luther once said he wished he could pray as this dog looks at the meat. On what are you focusing? What is your god?

Are you ready to let go of the journal, the spoken prayers, music and the rest? For today, go on a walk with nothing in your hands. Just you, God and the world. Say nothing. Let your mind be at rest and at peace with God. Let God be the prayer.

40

Now What?

Let anyone who is thirsty come to me, and let the one who believes in me drink. As the scripture has said, "Out of the believer's heart shall flow rivers of living water."

—John 7:37b-38

So now what?

You could go back to the beginning and start over again. You could skip some chapters and spend several days or even weeks on others.

Or, go back over the chapters of this book and circle the ones that spoke to you. Pick one or two that left you wanting more and spend some time drinking from those wells. In the future, if those wells run dry, pick some others to jump start your prayer life and quench your soul.

Consult your pastor or visit a spiritual director. Find a spiritual coach that you trust, someone who has been down this road.

Don't lose the prayer pattern you've established. Schedule the time you carved out that worked the best, where you stuck with it the longest. You have your whole life ahead of you. Walk with God. Drink deeply of the Spirit. This life is more than work, and food, and things. The most important things are the intangibles: love, joy, peace, patience, kindness. Kindle the fire of love.

"By this everyone will know that you are my disciples, if you have love for one another." (John 13:35) Filled with the Spirit, go into the world "and live in love, as Christ loved us and gave himself up for us, a fragrant offering and sacrifice to God." (Ephesians 5:2)

Then return to the silence. Where God waits. Offering gifts of peace, joy, hope and love.

> *Jesus said to them, "Come away to a deserted place all by yourselves and rest a while…"*
>
> —Mark 6:31

> *The fruit of silence is prayer*
> *the fruit of prayer is faith*
> *the fruit of faith is love*
> *the fruit of love is service*
> *the fruit of service is peace.*
>
> —Mother Teresa

Appendix A:

A Prayer for Each Month

Some of these are liturgical prayers. They will feed your prayer life and connect it to the prayers of the assembly.

January - This prayer comes from the a baptismal liturgy. I chose it for this month since January is the Baptism of our Lord, and a great time for Affirmation of Baptism. I chose it in general because it is a prayer we pray at every baptism, with hands laid on the baptized. It's a good prayer to know by heart, since we enter the life of faith through baptism.

We give you thanks, O God, that through water and the Holy Spirit you give your daughters and sons new birth, cleanse them from sin, and raise them to eternal life. Sustain us/name with the gift of your Holy Spirit: the spirit of wisdom and understanding, the spirit of counsel and might, the spirit of knowledge and the fear of the Lord, the spirit of joy in your presence, both now and forever. Amen.

February - This is a prayer of faith and courage in new ventures.

Lord God, you have called your servants to new ventures of which we cannot see the ending, by paths as yet untrod, through perils unknown. Give is faith to go out with courage, not knowing where we go, but only that your hand is leading us and your love is supporting us, through Jesus Christ our Lord. Amen.

March - From St. Patrick's Breastplate:

Christ with me, Christ before me, Christ behind me,
Christ in me, Christ beneath me, Christ above me,
Christ on my right, Christ on my left,
Christ when I lie down, Christ when I sit down, Christ when I arise,

Christ in the heart of everyone who thinks of me,
Christ in the mouth of everyone who speaks of me,
Christ in every eye that sees me,
Christ in every ear that hears me.
I arise today
Through a mighty strength, the invocation of the Trinity,
Through belief in the threeness,
Through confession of the oneness,
Of the Creator of Creation. Amen.

April - This is the Proper Preface for Easter.

It is indeed right, our duty and our joy, that we should at all times
and in all places offer thanks and praise to you Almighty God. But
chiefly are we bound to praise you for the glorious resurrection of
your Son Jesus Christ our Lord; for he is the true Paschal Lamb,
who was sacrificed for us, and has taken away the sin of the world.
By his death he has destroyed death, and by his rising to life again
he has won for us eternal life.

And so with Mary Magdalene and Peter, and all the witnesses of the
resurrection, with angels and archangels and all the company of
heaven, we praise your name and join their unending hymn:

Holy, holy, holy, lord God of power and might, heaven and earth are
full of your glory. Hosanna in the highest. Blessed is the one who
comes in the name of the Lord. Hosanna in the highest.

May - This prayer comes from the service of Affirmation of
Baptism. It is the prayer said over every confirmand with the laying
on of hands. I chose it for May because many congregations
celebrate the Rite of Confirmation in May. It is a good prayer to
have committed to memory, both devotionally and liturgically.

Father in heaven, for Jesus' sake, stir up in us the gift of your Holy
Spirit; confirm our faith, guide our lives, empower us in our serving,
give us patience in suffering, and bring us to everlasting life. Amen.

June - Luther's morning prayer:

In the name of the Father and of the Son and of the Holy Spirit. Amen. I thank you, my heavenly Father, through Jesus Christ, Your dear Son, that You have kept me this night from all harm and danger; and I pray that You would keep me this day also from sin and every evil, that all my doings in life may please You. For into Your hands I commend myself, my body and soul, and all things. Let Your holy angels be with me, that the evil foe may have no power over me. Amen.

July - This is a prayer that has always meant a lot to me personally at the beginning of the day.

Almighty and everlasting God, you have brought us in safety to this new day. Preserve us with your mighty power that we may not fall into sin, nor be overcome with adversity, and in all we do direct us to the fulfilling of your purpose, through Jesus Christ our Lord. Amen.

August - Prayer of St. Richard.

Thanks be to you, our Lord Jesus Christ, for all the benefits which you have given us, for all the pains and insults which you have borne for us. Most merciful Redeemer, Friend and Brother, may we know you more clearly, Love you more dearly, and follow you more nearly, day by day. Amen.

September - This is the Serenity Prayer, by Reinhold Niebuhr.

God, grant me the serenity to accept the things I cannot change, the courage to change the things I can, and the wisdom to know the difference. Amen.

October - A Prayer of St. Francis.

Lord, make me an instrument of your peace.
Where there is hatred, let me sow love.
Where there is injury, pardon.

Where there is doubt, faith.
Where there is despair, hope.
Where there is darkness, light.
Where there is sadness, joy.
O Divine Master,
grant that I may not so much seek to be consoled, as to console;
to be understood, as to understand;
to be loved, as to love.
For it is in giving that we receive.
It is in pardoning that we are pardoned,
and it is in dying that we are born to Eternal Life.
Amen.

November - I chose this Thomas Cranmer prayer for the last month of the church year, because of its sense of *teleos*.

Support us, Lord, all the day long, until the shadows lengthen, and the evening comes, the busy world is hushed, the fever of life is over, and our work is done; then Lord, in your mercy, give us safe lodging, a holy rest and peace at the last. Amen.

December - This is the Proper Preface for Christmas. It is a beloved incarnational prayer, and one that is handy to have memorized on Christmas Eve.

It is indeed right, our duty and our joy, that we should at all times and in all places offer thanks and praise to you Almighty God. "In the wonder and mystery of the Word made flesh you have opened the eyes of faith to a new and radiant vision of your glory; that, beholding the God made visible, we may be drawn to love the God whom we cannot see."

And so, with Angels and Archangels, and all the company of heaven, we praise your name and join their unending hymn:

Holy, holy, holy, lord God of power and might, heaven and earth are full of your glory. Hosanna in the highest. Blessed is the one who comes in the name of the Lord. Hosanna in the highest.

Appendix B:

Engaging Prayer in a Small Group Study or a Lenten Series

If you wish to use this book as a small group study, follow the outline below. Encourage your group(s) to download and read one chapter of the book each day. Each session begins with a prayer and Scripture reading, followed by a time to check in with your group about how you experienced the prayers during the last week. The group time is wrapped up with one of the forms of prayer.

There are 40 chapters. Invite people to read one a day. These chapters are appropriate for Lent (the 40 day period just prior to Easter). The three disciplines of Lent are prayer, fasting and almsgiving (generosity). All three of these are covered in the book. Those who want to use this for a Lenten series with worship can use one of the topics and scriptures from the first seven chapters for week one, one of the topics and scriptures from the second seven chapters for week two and so on. If small groups are not going to be part of the Lenten series, the small group sessions could be adapted, incorporating music from the prayer section of your hymnal or worship repertoire. Give people time to interact. If this is not practical in your congregation's context, consider providing a time for small group discussion afterward. People will internalize things better if they have a chance to process what they are experiencing and bounce ideas off others.

Small Group Outline:

1. Prayer – Begin with a short prayer to get people centered.

2. Scripture – Choose two of the Scriptures from the last seven days of readings.

3. Check-in – Give people an opportunity to share their reflections on the reading, and their experiences with the prayer exercises.

4. Prayer – Pick one of the prayer exercises to do as a group: *Lectio Divina,* prayer stations, the map prayer, stations of the cross, confession and absolution with dissolving paper, burning paper, or nailing paper to a cross, etc.

Week 1: Prior to this session read chapters 1-7.

Week 2: Prior to this session read chapters 8-14.

Week 3: Prior to this session read chapters 15-21.

Week 4: Prior to this session read chapters 22-28.

Week 5: Prior to this session read chapters 29-35.

Week 6: Prior to this session read chapters 36-40.

17700003R00057

Made in the USA
Middletown, DE
05 February 2015